French Love Poems

french
love
poems

Edited by Tynan Kogane

A New Directions Paperbook

Manufactured in the United States of America
New Directions Books are printed on acid-free paper
First published as a New Directions Paperbook in 2016
Design by Marian Bantjes

Library of Congress Cataloging-in-Publication Data
Names: Kogane, Tynan, 1985- editor.
Title: French love poems / edited by Tynan Kogane.
Description: First edition. | New York : New Directions Publishing
Corporation, 2016. | Parallel verses in English and French.
Identifiers: LCCN 2016017793 | ISBN 9780811225595 (alk. paper)
Subjects: LCSH: Love poetry, French. | Love poetry, French—Translations
into English.
Classification: LCC PQ1170.E6 F684 2016 | DDC 841.008/03543—dc23
LC record available at https://lccn.loc.gov/2016017793

10 9 8 7 6 5 4

New Directions Books are published for James Laughlin
by New Directions Publishing Corporation
80 Eighth Avenue, New York 10011

Table of Contents

Chanson de la plus haute tour

Qu'il vienne, qu'il vienne,
Le temps dont on s'éprenne.

J'ai tant fait patience
Qu'à jamais j'oublie.
Craintes et souffrances
Aux cieux sont parties.
Et la soif malsaine
Obscurcit mes veines.

Qu'il vienne, qu'il vienne,
Le temps dont on s'éprenne.

Telle la prairie
A l'oubli livrée,
Grandie et fleurie
D'encens et d'ivraies,
Au bourdon farouche
De sales mouches.

Qu'il vienne, qu'il vienne,
Le temps dont on s'éprenne.

Song of the Highest Tower

May it come, may it come,
The time when love astounds us.

I have kept so patient
That forever I forget.
Fears and sufferings
To the heavens have risen.
And the degenerate thirst
Darkens my veins.

May it come, may it come,
The time when love astounds us.

Like the meadow,
Left unattended,
Overgrown, florid
With fragrance and rye,
Amid the harsh hum
Of dirty flies.

May it come, may it come,
The time when love astounds us.

Translated by
Delmore Schwartz

CHARLES BAUDELAIRE (1821–1867)

Les bijoux

La très-chère était nue, et, connaissant mon cœur,
Elle n'avait gardé que ses bijoux sonores,
Dont le riche attirail lui donnait l'air vainqueur
Qu'ont dans leurs jours heureux les esclaves des Mores.

Quand il jette en dansant son bruit vif et moqueur,
Ce monde rayonnant de métal et de pierre
Me ravit en extase, et j'aime à la fureur
Les choses où le son se mêle à la lumière.

Elle était donc couchée et se laissait aimer,
Et du haut du divan elle souriait d'aise
A mon amour profond et doux comme la mer,
Qui vers elle montait comme vers sa falaise.

Les yeux fixés sur moi, comme un tigre dompté,
D'un air vague et rêveur elle essayait des poses,
Et la candeur unie à la lubricité
Donnait un charme neuf à ses métamorphoses;

Et son bras et sa jambe, et sa cuisse et ses reins,
Polis comme de l'huile, onduleux comme un cygne,
Passaient devant mes yeux clairvoyants et sereins;
Et son ventre et ses seins, ces grappes de ma vigne,

Jewels

The darling one was naked and, knowing my wish,
Had kept only the regalia of her jewelry
Whose resonant charms can lure and vanquish
Like a Moorish slave-girl's in her moment of glory.

A world of dazzling stones and of precious metals
Flinging, in its quick rhythm, glints of mockery
Ravishes me into ecstasy, I love to madness
The mingling of sounds and lights in one intricacy.

Naked, then, she was to all of my worship,
Smiling in triumph from the heights of her couch
At my desire advancing, as gentle and deep
As the sea sending its waves to the warm beach.

Her eyes fixed as a tiger's in the tamer's trance,
Absent, unthinking, she varied her poses
With an audacity and wild innocence
That gave a strange pang to each metamorphosis.

Her long legs, her hips, shining smooth as oil,
Her arms and her thighs, undulant as a swan,
Lured my serene, clairvoyant gaze to travel
To her belly and breasts, the grapes of my vine.

S'avançaient, plus câlins que les Anges du mal,
Pour troubler le repos où mon âme était mise,
Et pour la déranger du rocher de cristal
Où, calme et solitaire, elle s'était assise.

Je croyais voir unis par un nouveau dessin
Les hanches de l'Antiope au buste d'un imberbe,
Tant sa taille faisait ressortir son bassin.
Sur ce teint fauve et brun le fard était superbe!

—Et la lampe s'étant résignée à mourir,
Comme le foyer seul illuminait la chambre,
Chaque fois qu'il poussait un flamboyant soupir,
Il inondait de sang cette peau couleur d'ambre!

With a charm as powerful as an evil angel
To trouble the calm where my soul had retreated,
They advanced slowly to dislodge it from its crystal
Rock, where its loneliness meditated.

With the hips of Antiope, the torso of a boy,
So deeply was the one form sprung into the other
It seemed as if desire had fashioned a new toy.
Her farded, fawn-brown skin was perfection to either!

—And the lamp having at last resigned itself to death,
There was nothing now but firelight in the room,
And every time a flame uttered a gasp for breath
It flushed her amber skin with the blood of its bloom.

Translated by David Paul

Sonnet XVIII

Baise m'encor, rebaise moy & baise:
Donne m'en un de tes plus savoureus,
Donne m'en un de tes plus amoureus:
Je t'en rendray quatre plus chaus que braise.

Las, te pleins tu? ça que ce mal j'apaise,
En t'en donnant dix autres doucereus.
Ainsi meslans nos baisers tant heureus
Jouissons nous l'un de l'autre à notre aise.

Lors double vie à chacun en suivra.
Chacun en soy & son ami vivra.
Permets m'Amour penser quelque folie:

Tousjours suis mal, vivant discrettement,
Et ne me puis donner contentement,
Si hors de moy ne fay quelque saillie.

Sonnet XVIII

Kiss me, rekiss me, & kiss me again:
Give me one of your most delicious kisses,
A kiss in excess of my fondest wishes:
I'll repay you four, more scalding than you spend.

You complain? Well, let me ease your pain
By giving you ten more honeyed kisses.
And as kiss with kiss so happily mixes,
Let's ease back into our shared joy again.

Then a double life to each shall ensue.
Each shall live: you in me, & me in you.
Love, something crazy comes to mind:

I can't bear living on my best behavior,
And there's no joy I could truly savor,
Unless aroused to leave myself behind.

Translated by Richard Sieburth

L'amante

Tant la passion m'avait saisi pour cette amante délectable, moi non exempt d'épanchement et d'oscillante lubricité, je devais, ne devais pas mourir en sourdine ou modifié, reconnu des seules paupières de mon amante. Les nuits de nouveauté sauvage avaient retrouvé l'ardente salive communicante, et parfumé son appartenance fiévreuse. Mille précautions altérées me conviaient à la plus voluptueuse chair qui soit. À nos mains un désir d'outre destin, quelle crainte à nos lèvres demain?

The Lover

I'd been so seized by passion for this delectable lover.
I not exactly exempt from feeling, from tremblors of lust. It
meant I must, meant I absolutely must not, just fade away
quietly, mildly changed, recognized only by the eyelids of
my lover. Nights of savage newness found for me again
the flaming saliva that connects and perfumed the fevered
connection. A thousand precautions gave way thirstily to
the most voluptuous flesh there could be. In our hands
desire that transcends. What fear on our lips tomorrow?

Translated by Frederick Seidel

Les roses de Saadi

J'ai voulu ce matin te rapporter des roses;
Mais j'en avais tant pris dans mes ceintures closes
Que les nœuds trop serrés n'ont pu les contenir.

Les nœuds ont éclaté. Les roses envolées
Dans le vent, à la mer s'en sont toutes allées.
Elles ont suivi l'eau pour ne plus revenir;

La vague en a paru rouge et comme enflammée.
Ce soir, ma robe encore en est toute embaumée…
Respires-en sur moi l'odorant souvenir.

The Roses of Saadi

I wanted to bring you roses this morning.
There were so many I wanted to bring,
The knots at my waist could not hold so many.

The knots burst. All the roses took wing,
The air was filled with roses flying,
Carried by the wind, into the sea.

The waves are red, as though they are burning.
My dress still has the scent of the morning,
Remembering roses. Smell them on me.

Translated by Louis Simpson

Couvre-feu

Que voulez-vous la porte était gardée
Que voulez-vous nous étions enfermés
Que voulez-vous la rue était barrée
Que voulez-vous la ville était matée
Que voulez-vous elle était affamée
Que voulez-vous nous étions désarmés
Que voulez-vous la nuit était tombée
Que voulez-vous nous nous sommes aimés.

Curfew

So what the door was guarded
So what we were imprisoned there
So what the street was barred off
So what the town was under attack
So what she was famished
So what we were without arms
So what night had fallen
So what we made love.

Translated by William Carlos Williams

Autre éventail

de Mademoiselle Mallarmé

O rêveuse, pour que je plonge
Au pur délice sans chemin,
Sache, par un subtil mensonge,
Garder mon aile dans ta main.

Une fraîcheur de crépuscule
Te vient à chaque battement
Dont le coup prisonnier recule
L'horizon délicatement.

Vertige! voici que frissonne
L'espace comme un grand baiser
Qui, fou de naître pour personne,
Ne peut jaillir ni s'apaiser.

Sens-tu le paradis farouche
Ainsi qu'un rire enseveli
Se couler du coin de ta bouche
Au fond de l'unanime pli!

Le sceptre des rivages roses
Stagnants sur les soirs d'or, ce l'est,
Ce blanc vol fermé que tu poses
Contre le feu d'un bracelet.

Another Fan

of Mademoiselle Mallarmé

Oh dreamer, that I may plunge
Pathless to pure delight,
Learn by a subtle lie
To keep my wing in your hand.

A twilight coolness comes
Upon you with each beat
Whose caged stroke lightly
Thrusts the horizon back.

Now feel space shivering
Dizzy, some great kiss
Which, wild to be born in vain,
Cannot break forth or rest.

Can you feel paradise
Shy as a buried laugh, slip
From the corner of your mouth
Down the concerted fold!

The scepter of pink shores
Stagnant on the golden eves is
This white shut slight you pose
Against a bracelet's fire.

Translated by
Peter and Mary Ann Caws

Nyx

O vous mes nuits, ô noires attendues
O pays fier, ô secrets obstinés
O longs regards, ô foudroyantes nues
O vol permis outre les cieux fermés.

O grand désir, ô surprise épandue
O beau parcours de l'esprit enchanté
O pire mal, ô grâce descendue
O porte ouverte ou nul n'avait passé

Je ne sais pas pourquoi je meurs et noie
Avant d'entrer à l'éternel séjour.
Je ne sais pas de qui je suis la proie.
Je ne sais pas de qui je suis l'amour.

Nyx

Oh you my nights, oh awaited darks
Oh proud country, oh stubborn secrets
Oh long looks, oh thundering clouds
Oh flight allowed beyond closed skies.

Oh great desire, oh spilled surprise
Oh lovely course of enchanted mind
Oh worse evil, oh grace descended
Oh open door where no one went

I know not why I die and drown
Before entering eternal rest.
I know not whose prey I am.
I know not whose love I am.

Translated by Mary Ann Caws

MAURICE SCÈVE (c. 1500–1564)

"Asses plus long, qu'un Siecle Platonique"

Asses plus long, qu'un Siecle Platonique,
Me fut le moys, que sans toy suis esté:
Mais quand ton front ie reuy pacifique,
Seiour treshault de toute honnesteté,
Ou l'empire est du conseil arresté
Mes songes lors ie creus ester deuins.
     Car en mon corps: mon Ame, tu reuins,
Sentant ses mains, mains celestement blanches,
Auec leurs bras mortellement diuins
L'un coronner mon col, l'aultre mes hanches.

"Far longer than a Platonic Year"

Far longer than a Platonic Year
The month I lived without you:
But again seeing your peaceful face,
Highest dwelling of noble grace,
Beyond anything reason might appraise,
I believed my dreams were prophecies.

    For into my body: my soul, you returned,
Feeling her hands, hands heavenly white,
With their arms, both mortally divine,
One crowning my neck, the other my thighs.

Translated by Richard Sieburth

JOYCE MANSOUR (1928–1986)

"Vous ne connaissez pas mon visage de nuit"

Vous ne connaissez pas mon visage de nuit
Mes yeux tels des chevaux fous d'espace
Ma bouche bariolée de sang inconnu
Ma peau
Mes doigts poteaux indicateurs perlés de plaisir
Guideront vos cils vers mes oreilles mes omoplates
Vers la campagne ouverte de ma chair
Les gradins de mes côtes se resserrent à l'idée
Que votre voix pourrait remplir ma gorge
Que vos yeux pourraient sourire
Vous ne connaissez pas la pâleur de mes épaules
La nuit
Quand les flammes hallucinantes des cauchemars
    réclament le silence
Et que les murs mous de la réalité s'étreignent
Vous ne savez pas que les parfums de mes journées
    meurent sur ma langue
Quand viennent les malins aux couteaux flottants
Que seul reste mon amour hautain
Quand je m'enfonce dans la boue de la nuit

"You do not know my face at night"

You do not know my face at night
My eyes like space-wild horses
My mouth varicolored with unknown blood
My skin
My fingers guideposts pearled with pleasure
Will lead your lashes toward my ears and shoulder blades
Toward the open country of my flesh
The bleachers of my ribs contract at the idea
That your voice could fill my throat
That your eyes could smile
You don't know the paleness of my shoulders
At night
When the raving flames of nightmares reclaim the
    silence
And when the soft walls of reality embrace
You don't know how the perfumes of my days are dying
    on my tongue
When the bad guys with the floating knives
May only my haughty love remain
When I sink down into the mud of night

Translated by Mary Ann Caws

En sourdine

Calmes dans le demi-jour
Que les branches hautes font,
Pénétrons bien notre amour
De ce silence profond.

Fondons nos âmes, nos cœurs
Et nos sens extasiés,
Parmi les vagues langueurs
Des pins et des arbousiers.

Ferme tes yeux à demi,
Croise tes bras sur ton sein,
Et de ton cœur endormi
Chasse à jamais tout dessein.

Laissons-nous persuader
Au souffle berceur et doux
Qui vient à tes pieds rider
Les ondes de gazon roux.

Et quand, solennel, le soir
Des chênes noirs tombera,
Voix de notre désespoir,
Le rossignol chantera.

Sourdine

Calm in the half-day
Where deep branches abound,
Let us mingle our love
With silence profound.

Let us melt our two souls
In ecstasy fine
With the vague langours
Of shrub and of pine.

Half close your eyes,
Cross your arms on your breast,
With the heart sleeping,
Peacefully rest.

Welcome the breathing wind
That is rippling so sweet
The waves of red grasses
That move at your feet.

And, when the dim twilight
Solemnly falls,
Voice of our sorrow
The nightingale calls.

Translated by
Bergen Applegate

JEAN JOUBERT (1928–2015)

Eau de lune

L'œil aiguisé
par ton
visage

j'ai vu au soir
la mer
violette

l'appel des
feux

puis l'eau
de
lune

Moonwater

With eyes made keen
by watching your face

I've seen at dusk
the sea
      violet

the beckoning
   points of light

then:
    moonwater.

Translated by Denise Levertov

ANNA DE NOAILLES (1876–1933)

"L'être ne recherche que soi"

L'être ne recherche que soi
A travers le multiple choix
De l'amour et de ses orages.
O Désir, somptueux voyage
Vers notre fascinante image
Qui nous exalte ou nous déçoit!
—C'est à soi-même qu'on veut plaire
Sur le cœur brûlant qui nous plaît,
Où, dans l'ivresse et la colère,
Ne sachent si l'on aime ou hait,
Par la volupté l'on espère
Mourir, et ne mourir jamais!

"It is ourselves we long to find"

It is ourselves we long to find
From within the countless binds
Of love and all its wreckage.
Desire, that magnificent voyage
Toward our own enthralling image
That disappoints or glorifies!
—It is ourselves we aim to please
Resting on the burning heart of another,
Where, in rage and ecstasy,
Whether we love or hate we can't remember,
Through our lust we hope, we seek
To die, and live forever!

Translated by Emma Ramadan

JACQUES PRÉVERT (1900–1977)

Alicante

Une orange sur la table
Ta robe sur le tapis
Et toi dans mon lit
Doux présent de la présent
Fraîcheur de la nuit
Chaleur de ma vie

Alicante

An orange on the table
Your dress on the rug
And you in my bed
Sweet present of the present
Cool of night
Warmth of my life.

Translated by Lawrence Ferlinghetti

ARTHUR RIMBAUD (1854–1891)

Première soirée

—Elle était fort déshabillée
Et de grands arbres indiscrets
Aux vitres jetaient leur feuillée
Malinement, tout près, tout près.

Assise sur ma grande chaise,
Mi-nue, elle joignait les mains.
Sur le plancher frissonnaient d'aise
Ses petits pieds si fins, si fins.

—Je regardai, couleur de cire,
Un petit rayon buissonnier
Papillonner dans son sourire
Et sur son sein, —mouche au rosier.

—Je baisai ses fines chevilles.
Elle eut un doux rire brutal
Qui s'égrenait en claires trilles,
Un joli rire de cristal.

Les petits pieds sous la chemise
Se sauvèrent: "Veux-tu finir!"
—La première audace permise,
Le rire feignait de punir!

Comedy in Three Caresses

She hadn't much left on, and the big trees,
With no discretion, swished
Their leaves over the window-pane
Teasingly, so near, so near.

Half naked in my big chair,
She put her hands together
And her little toes tickled the floor,
Quivering comfortably, and so small.

I watched a little sprouting flush,
The color of wax, flutter
Like a smile over her neat breasts:
Fly on a rose bush.

I kissed her traced ankles
And she smiled a longish smile, bad sign
That shattered out into clear trills,
Crystalline.

Her little feet scampered under her shift:
"Will you *stop* now!!"
After the first permitted boldness,
The smile pretending coldness?

—Pauvrets palpitants sous ma lèvre,
Je baisai doucement ses yeux:
—Elle jeta sa tête mièvre
En arrière: "Oh! c'est encor mieux!…

Monsieur, j'ai deux mots à te dire…"
—Je lui jetai le reste au sein
Dans un baiser, qui la fit rire
D'un bon rire qui voulait bien…

—Elle était fort déshabillée
Et de grands arbres indiscrets
Aux vitres jetaient leur feuillée
Malinement, tout près, tout près.

Her poor eyelids fluttered under my lips
As I kissed her eyes
And she threw back her weakling head:
"That's better now," she said.

"But I have something still to …"
I chucked the rest between her breasts
In a caress that brought a kindly smile,
Benevolence, all of it.

She hadn't much left on, and the big trees
Swished their leaves over the window-pane
At ease, teasingly, and so near.

Translated by Ezra Pound

CLAUDE CAHUN (1894–1954)

Self-Love

Une main crispée sur un miroir—une bouche, des narines palpitantes—entre des paupières pamées, la fixité folle de prunelles élargies … Dans l'horizon brutal d'une lampe électrique, en blond, mauve et vert sous les étoiles, voilà tout, par pudeur! ce que je voudrais éclairer du mystère: le néo-narcissisme d'une humanité pratique.

Mon tableau serait de cette époque hypocrite et sensuelle où les hommes préféreront leur propre contact et son muet mépris à l'amour bavard des autres.

Croirait-on la chose impossible? On oppose à ce tableau les morales et les autres amours. Pourtant le tain des miroirs épaissit. Non plus absolu, mais aimablement relatif, l'être s'individualise. L'orgueil devient vertu. Le corps se connaît et s'absout.

Le mythe de Narcisse est partout. Il nous hante. Il a sans cesse inspiré ce qui perfectionne la vie, depuis le jour fatal où fut captée l'onde sans ride. Car l'invention du métal poli est d'une claire étymologie narcissienne.

Self-Love

A hand clutching a mirror—a mouth, two quivering nostrils—between faint eyelids, the mad fixity of enlarged pupils … In the brutal sweep of an electric lamp, blond, mauve and green under the stars, that's all there is, modestly! What I would like to clarify from the mystery: the neo-narcissism of a practical humanity.

My painting would represent this hypocritical and sensual epoch in which people prefer their own contact and its mute scorn for the talkative love of others.

Does this seem impossible? We oppose morals and other loves to this picture. However the silvering of mirrors thickens. No longer absolute, but wonderfully relative, the person is individualized. Pride becomes virtue. The body knows and absolves itself.

The myth of Narcissus is everywhere. It haunts us. Doubtless it has inspired what makes life perfect, from the fatal day when the unwrinkled wave was caught. For the invention of polished metal is of a clearly narcissist etymology.

Le bronze—l'argent—le verre: nos miroirs sont presque parfaits. Nous souffrons encore de leur position verticale; c'est déjà plus confortable qu'un plat-ventre sur le gazon. Les paresseux étendus sur leur ombre se mirent dans le ciel. Mais pour peu qu'un fâcheux les tire de leur mollesse, avec un bruit de verre cassé le reflet se brise.

Il faudrait maintenant fixer l'image dans le temps comme dans l'espace, saisir des mouvements accomplis—se surprendre de dos enfin.

« Miroir », « fixer », voilà des mots qui n'ont rein à faire ici.

En somme, ce qui gêne le plus Narcisse le voyeur, c'est l'insuffisance, la discontinuité de son propre regard.

Bronze—silver—glass: our mirrors are almost perfect. We suffer still from their vertical position; it's already more comfortable than being extended on the lawn. The lazy ones stretched out on their shadow gaze at themselves in the sky. But if someone meddlesome draws them out of their softness, the reflection breaks apart with a noise of broken glass.

Now we should fix the image in time as in space, seize the motions completed—finally surprise ourselves from behind.

"Mirror," "to fix," these words are out of place here.

Finally what worries Narcissus the voyeur the most is the insufficiency, the discontinuity of his own gaze.

Translated by Mary Ann Caws

ANDRÉ BRETON (1896–1966)

Yeux zinzolins

Yeux zinzolins de la petite Babylonienne trop blanche
Au nombril sertissant une pierre de même couleur
Quand s'ouvre comme une croisée sur un jardin nocturne
La main de Jacqueline X
Que vous êtes pernicieux au fond de cette main
Yeux d'outre-temps à jamais humides
Fleur qui pourriez vous appeler la réticence du prophète
C'en est fait du présent du passé de l'avenir
Je chante la lumière unique de la coïncidence
La joie de m'être penché sur la grande rosace du glacier
    supérieur
Les infiltrations merveilleuses dont on s'aperçoit un beau
    jour qu'elles ont fait un cornet du plancher
La portée des incidents étranges mais insignifiants à
    première vue
Et leur don d'appropriation finale vertigineuse à moi-
    même
Je chante votre horizon fatal
Vous qui clignez imperceptiblement dans la main de mon
    amour
Entre le rideau de vie
Et le rideau de cœur
Yeux zinzolins
Y Z
De l'alphabet secret de toute-nécessité

Violet Eyes

Violet eyes of the tiny, too white Babylonian girl
With the navel setting a stone of the same color
When, like a window on a garden at night
The hand of Jacqueline X opens
How pernicious you are in the hollow of that hand
Ever-wet eyes beyond time
Flower you might be called the reticence of the prophet
And there's an end of picturing the past and the future
I sing the unique light of coincidence
The joy of having leaned over the great rose window of
     the far glacier
The marvelous infiltrations one discovers one fine day
     when they have made a horn of the ceiling
The compass of strange incidents, strange but
     insignificant at first glance
And their gift of finally, dizzily appropriating all of me
I sing your fatal horizon
You who blink imperceptibly in the hand of my love
Between the curtain of life
And the curtain of heart
Violet eyes
V E
Of the secret alphabet of entire necessity

Translated by
Wayne Andrews

CHARLES BAUDELAIRE (1821–1867)

Le serpent qui danse

Que j'aime voir, chère indolente,
    De ton corps si beau,
Comme une étoffe vacillante,
    Miroiter la peau!

Sur ta chevelure profonde
    Aux âcres parfums,
Mer odorante et vagabonde
    Aux flots bleus et bruns,

Comme un navire qui s'éveille
    Au vent du matin,
Mon âme rêveuse appareille
    Pour un ciel lointain.

Tes yeux, où rien ne se révèle
    De doux ni d'amer,
Sont deux bijoux froids où se mêle
    L'or avec le fer.

A te voir marcher en cadence,
    Belle d'abandon,
On dirait un serpent qui danse
    Au bout d'un bâton.

The Dancing Serpent

Dear indolent, I love to see,
    In your body bright,
How like shimmering silk the skin
    Reflects the light!

On the deep ocean of your hair
    Where perfume laves,
Odorous and vagabond sea
    Of blue and brown waves,

Like a vessel awakening
    When morning winds rise
My dreaming soul begins to sail
    Toward remote skies.

Your two eyes that neither sweetness
    Nor bitterness hold
Are two chilly gems mingled of
    Iron and gold.

When you walk in rhythm, lovely
    With abandonment,
You seem to be swayed by a wand,
    A dancing serpent.

Sous le fardeau de ta paresse
    Ta tête d'enfant
Se balance avec la mollesse
    D'un jeune éléphant,

Et ton corps se penche et s'allonge
    Comme un fin vaisseau
Qui roule bord sur bord et plonge
    Ses vergues dans l'eau.

Comme un flot grossi par la fonte
    Des glaciers grondants,
Quand l'eau de ta bouche remonte
    Au bord de tes dents,

Je crois boire un vin de Bohême,
    Amer et vainqueur,
Un ciel liquide qui parsème
    D'étoiles mon cœur!

Your child's head under the burden
   Of your indolence
Sways as delicately as a
   Young elephant's,

And your body bends and straightens
   Like a slender ship
That, plunging and rolling, lets the
   Yards in water dip.

When, like a stream by thawing of
   Glaciers made replete,
The water of your mouth rises
   Up to your teeth,

I drink a Bohemian wine,
   Powerful and tart,
A liquid sky that sows its stars
   Within my heart!

Translated by Barbara Gibbs

A***

Tu es mon amour depuis tant d'années,
Mon vertige devant tant d'attente,
Que rien ne peut vieillir, froidir;
Même ce qui attendait notre mort,
Ou lentement sut nous combattre,
Même ce qui nous est étranger,
Et mes éclipses et mes retours.

Fermée comme un volet de buis
Une extrême chance compacte
Est notre chaîne de montagnes,
Notre comprimante splendeur.

Je dis chance, ô ma martelée;
Chacun de nous peut recevoir
Le part de mystère de l'autre
Sans en répandre le secret;
Et la douleur qui vient d'ailleurs
Trouve enfin sa séparation
Dans la chair de notre unité,
Trouve enfin sa route solaire
Au centre de notre nuée
Qu'elle déchire et recommence.

To***

For years now you have been my love,
The vertigo I feel when I lie waiting
That nothing can make old, make cold;
Even that which was expecting our death,
Or gradually knew how to combat us,
Even that which we are strangers to,
My eclipses and also my returns.

Barred like a boxwood shutter,
And extreme and compact fortune
Is our mountain range,
Our compressing splendor.

I say fortune, o my wrought one;
Each of us can receive
Another's share of mystery
Without spilling its secret;
And the suffering that comes from elsewhere
Finds at last its separation
In the flesh of our unity,
Finds at last its solar road
At the center of our dense cloud
Which it tears and recommences.

Je dis chance comme je le sens.
Tu as élevé le sommet
Que devra franchir mon attente
Quand demain disparaîtra.

I say fortune the way I feel it.
You have raised the summit
That my waiting will have to cross
When tomorrow is no longer there.

Translated by Mark Hutchinson

de *Saint Graal*

Torrent d'amour du Dieu d'amour et de douceur,
Fût-ce parmi l'horreur de ce monde moqueur,
Fleuve rafraîchissant de feu qui désaltère,
Source vive où s'en vient ressusciter le cœur
Même de l'assassin, même de l'adultère,
Salut de la patrie, ô sang qui désaltère!

from **Saint Graal**

                         Torrent of love
from the God Himself Love and Sweetness,
Eternal Cup He is, we moved toward, even be it
amidst the horror of this mocking world we face,
refreshing river of fire that quenches thirst,
live source where the heart may be revived,
even of the assassin, even of the adulterer,
salvation of the fatherland, O blood, gift of love,
     that quenches life's thirst!

Translated by Robert Duncan

Epousailles

A une qui est au bord de l'Océan

L'amour a épousé l'absence, un soir d'été;
Si bien que mon amour pour votre adolescence
Accompagne à pas lents sa femme, votre absence,
Qui, très douce, le mène et, tranquille, se tait.
Et l'amour qui s'en vint aux bords océaniques,
Où le ciel serait grec si toutes étaient nues,
Y pleure d'être dieu encore et inconnu,
Ce dieu jaloux comme le sont les dieux uniques.

Wedding

To One who is at the Seashore

Love wed the absence of a summer night;
So much so that my love for your soft youth
Slowly accompanies its wife, your absence,
Who, sweet and tranquil, leads him and is still.
And love which went away to find the sea,
Where nudes would make the sky seem Greek,
Weeps to be still a god and still unknown,
A jealous god as only gods can be.

Translated by Roger Shattuck

RENÉE VIVIEN (1877–1909)

A la femme aimée

Lorsque tu vins, à pas réfléchis, dans la brume,
Le ciel mêlait aux ors le cristal et l'airain.
Ton corps se devinait, ondoiement incertain,
Plus souple que la vague et plus frais que l'écume.
Le soir d'été semblait un rêve oriental
De rose et de santal.

Je tremblais. De longs lys religieux et blêmes
Se mouraient dans tes mains, comme des cierges froids.
Leurs parfums expirants s'échappaient de tes doigts
En le souffle pâmé des angoisses suprêmes.
De tes clairs vêtements s'exhalaient tour à tour
L'agonie et l'amour.

Je sentis frissonner sur mes lèvres muettes
La douceur et l'effroi de ton premier baiser.
Sous tes pas, j'entendis les lyres se briser
En criant vers le ciel l'ennui fier des poètes
Parmi des flots de sons languissamment décrus,
Blonde, tu m'apparus.

To the Beloved Woman

When you came, with lingering steps, in the mist,
The heavens mingled crystal and bronze with gold.
Your body could be glimpsed dimly weaving,
Suppler than the wave, fresher than the foam.
The summer evening seemed an oriental dream
Of rose and sandalwood.

I was trembling. Tall white lilies sacred
Were perishing in your hands, like chill tapers.
Their scents were drifting from your fingers
In the exhausted breath of supreme anguish.
Your bright clothes were exhaling
Agony and love.

Shivering on my mute lips I felt
The sweetness and the fright of your first kiss.
Under your steps, I heard lyres breaking
Crying to the sky a poet's proud boredom
Among the floods of sound languishingly ebbed,
Blonde, you appeared to me.

Et l'esprit assoiffé d'éternel, d'impossible,
D'infini, je voulus moduler largement
Un hymne de magie et d'émerveillement.
Mais la strophe monta bégayante et pénible,
Reflet naïf, écho puéril, vol heurté,
Vers ta Divinité.

My spirit athirst for the eternal, the impossible,
The infinite, I wanted to compose at large
A hymn of magic and marveling.
But the verse rose stammering and pained,
Naïve image, childish echo, flight jolted
Toward your Divinity.

Translated by Mary Ann Caws

Les pas

Tes pas, enfants de mon silence,
Saintement, lentement placés,
Vers le lit de ma vigilance
Procèdent muets et glacés.

Personne pure, ombre divine,
Qu'ils sont doux, tes pas retenus!
Dieux!... tous les dons que je devine
Viennent à moi sur ces pieds nus!

Si, de tes lèvres avancées,
Tu prépares pour l'apaiser,
A l'habitant de mes pensées
La nourriture d'un baiser,

Ne hâte pas cet acte tendre,
Douceur d'être et de n'être pas,
Car j'ai vécu de vous attendre,
Et mon cœur n'était que vos pas.

The Footsteps

Born of my voiceless time, your steps
Slowly, ecstatically advance:
Toward my expectation's bed
They move in a hushed, ice-clear trance.

Pure being, shadow-shape divine—
Your step deliberate, how sweet!
God!—every gift I have imagined
Comes to me on those naked feet.

If so it be your offered mouth
Is shaped already to appease
That which occupied my thought
With the live substance of a kiss,

Oh hasten not this loving act,
Rapture where self and not-self meet:
My life has been the awaiting of you,
Your footfall was my own heart's beat.

Translated by C. Day Lewis

ANDRÉE CHEDID (1920–2011)

Preuves de l'amour

Gisement de désirs
Eperon du souffle

L'amour

Recouvre la fêlure
Soulève nos sols

Tisonne nos cendres
Estompe nos voûtes obscures.

Proofs of Love

Stratum of desires
Spur of the breath

Love

Recovers the crack
Raises our earths

Stirs our ashes
Blurs our dark vaults.

Translated by Mary Ann Caws

CHARLES BAUDELAIRE (1821–1867)

"Je t'adore a l'égal de la voûte nocturne"

Je t'adore à l'égal de la voûte nocturne,
O vase de tristesse, ô grande taciturne,
Et t'aime d'autant plus, belle, que tu me fuis,
Et que tu me parais, ornement de mes nuits,
Plus ironiquement accumuler les lieues
Qui séparent mes bras des immensités bleues.

Je m'avance à l'attaque, et je grimpe aux assauts,
Comme après un cadavre un chœur de vermisseaux,
Et je chéris, ô bête implacable et cruelle!
Jusqu'à cette froideur par où tu m'es plus belle!

"You, whom I worship as night's firmament"

You, whom I worship as night's firmament,
Urn of sorrow, beautiful and silent;
I love you more, because you turn from me
Adorning night, but, with large irony
Rather increase the absolute blue space
Which alienates the sky from my embrace.

I leap to your attack, climb in assault
Like corpseworms feeding nimbly in the vault,
And cherish you, relentless, cruel beast
Till that last coldness which delights me best.

Translated by Graham Reynolds

JOYCE MANSOUR (1928–1986)

Je veux dormir avec toi

Je veux dormir avec toi coude à coude
Cheveux entremêlés
Sexes noués
Avec ta bouche comme oreiller.
Je veux dormir avec toi dos à dos
Sans haleine pour nous séparer
Sans mots pour nous distraire
Sans yeux pour nous mentir
Sans vêtements.
Je veux dormir avec toi sein contre sein
Crispée et en sueur
Brillant de mille frissons
Mangée par l'inertie folle de l'extase
Ecartelée sur ton ombre
Martelée par ta langue
Pour mourir entre les dents cariées de lapin
Heureuse.

I Want to Sleep with You

I want to sleep with you side by side
Our hair intertwined
Our sexes joined
With your mouth for a pillow.
I want to sleep with you back to back
With no breath to part us
No words to distract us
No eyes to lie to us
With no clothes on.
To sleep with you breast to breast
Tense and sweating
Shining with a thousand quivers
Consumed by ecstatic mad inertia
Stretched out on your shadow
Hammered by your tongue
To die in a rabbit's rotting teeth
Happy.

Translated by Mary Ann Caws

Tu seras nue

Tu seras nue dans le salon aux vieilles choses,
fine comme un fuseau de roseau de lumière,
et, les jambes croisées, auprès du feu rose,
        tu écouteras l'hiver.

A tes pieds, je prendrai dans mes bras tes genoux.
Tu souriras, plus gracieuse qu'une branche d'osier,
et, posant mes cheveux à ta hanche douce,
        je pleurerai que tu sois si douce.

Nos regards orgueilleux se feront bons pour nous,
et, quand je baiserai ta gorge, tu baisseras
les yeux en souriant vers moi et laisseras
        fléchir ta nuque douce.

Puis, quand viendra la vieille servante malade et fidèle
frapper à la porte en nous disant: le dîner est servi,
tu auras un sursaut rougissant, et ta main frêle
        préparera ta robe grise.

Et tandis que le vent passera sous la porte,
que la pendule usée sonnera mal,
tu mettras tes jambes au parfum d'ivoire
        dans leurs petits étuis noirs.

You Will Be Naked

You will be naked in the parlor among the old things,
Slim as a reed spindle of light,
And, legs crossed before the rosy fire,
            You will listen to the winter.

At your feet, I will take your knees in my arms.
You will smile, more gracious than a willow branch,
And, laying my hair against your sweet thighs,
            I will weep because you are so good.

It will be good for us to be proud of each other.
And when I kiss your throat, you will kiss
My eyes, and smile at me, and bend
            Your gentle neck.

Then, when the old servant, ill and faithful,
Raps on the door and says, "Dinner is served,"
You will start, and blush, and your slender hand
            Will adjust your grey robe.

And while the wind comes under the door,
And the worn clock strikes the wrong time,
You will put your legs, perfumed with ivory,
            Back in their little black cases.

Translated by
Kenneth Rexroth

GUILLAUME APOLLINAIRE (1880–1918)

La tzigane

La tzigane savait d'avance
Nos deux vies barrées par les nuits
Nous lui dîmes adieu et puis
De ce puits sortit l'Espérance

L'amour lourd comme un ours privé
Dansa debout quand nous voulûmes
Et l'oiseau bleu perdit ses plumes
Et les mendiants leurs Ave

On sait très bien que l'on se damne
Mais l'espoir d'aimer en chemin
Nous fait penser main dans le main
A ce qu'a prédit la tzigane

The Gypsy

The gypsy knew ahead of time
Our secret night-imprisoned lives
We said good-bye to her and hope
Sprang without reason from that well

Love like a lugubrious bear
Danced upright at our slightest will
The blue-bird lost his lovely plumes
And all the mendicants their beads

You know when you have damned yourself
But hopes of love along the way
Make us think hand in hand of what
The gypsy once foretold us

Translated by Roger Shattuck

Le voyage innomé

Où est-ce qu'elle va
quand elle ferme ses

yeux lorsque nous fai-
sons le radada elle est

là a mon côté et elle
n'est pas là si je la

touche elle frémit mais
elle ne me dit rien un

jour je lui ai demandé
où elle voyageait cette

fois elle a souri et m'a
répondu ne t'inquiètes

pas je n'irai jamais loin
de toi le pays auquel je

rends visite est ce des
poèmes que tu m'as écrit.

The Nameless Voyage

Where does she go
when she closes her eyes
when we are making love?

She is there by my side
yet she isn't there

If I touch her she trembles
but says nothing

One night I asked her
where it was she traveled

This time she smiled and answered
don't be worried
I'll never be far from you

The land that I visit
is the land of the poems
you have written for me.

Sonnet

Je ne vous ferai pas de vers,
Madame, blonde entre les blondes,
Vous réduiriez trop l'univers,
Vous seriez reine sur les mondes.

Vos yeux de saphir, grands ouverts,
Inquiètent comme les ondes
Des fleuves, des lacs et des mers
Et j'en ai des rages profondes.

Mais je suis pourtant désarmé
Par la bouche, rose de mai,
Qui parle si bien sans parole,

Et qui dit le mot sans pareil,
Fleur délicieusement folle
Eclose à Paris, au soleil.

Sonnet

I will not make verses for you,
Lady, blondest of blondes.
You will conquer enough of the universe,
You will be queen of all the worlds.

Your sapphire eyes, wide open,
Restless as the waves
Of the rivers, the lakes, and the sea,
Drive me crazy.

And I am always defenseless before
That mouth, rose of May,
Which says so much without words,

Which says the unmatchable word,
That flower deliciously wanton,
Blooming in Paris in the sun.

Translated by Kenneth Rexroth

PAUL ÉLUARD (1895–1952)

L'amoureuse

Elle est debout sur mes paupières
Et ses cheveux sont dans les miens,
Elle a la forme de mes mains,
Elle a la couleur de mes yeux,
Elle s'engloutit dans mon ombre
Comme une pierre sur le ciel.

Elle a toujours les yeux ouverts
Et ne me laisse pas dormir.
Ses rêves en pleine lumière
Font s'évaporer les soleils,
Me font rire, pleurer et rire,
Parler sans avoir rien à dire.

Woman in Love

She is standing on my eyelids
And her hair is in mine,
She has the shape of my hands,
She has the color of my eyes,
She is engulfed in my shadow
Like a stone against the sky.

Her eyes are always open
She does not let me sleep.
Her dreams in broad daylight
Make suns evaporate,
Make me laugh, weep and laugh,
And speak without anything to say.

Translated by Lloyd Alexander

Le Pont Mirabeau

Sous le pont Mirabeau coule la Seine
  Et nos amours
 Faut-il qu'il m'en souvienne
La joie venait toujours après la peine

  Vienne la nuit sonne l'heure
  Les jours s'en vont je demeure

Les mains dans les mains restons face à face
  Tandis que sous
 Le pont de nos bras passe
Des éternels regards l'onde si lasse

  Vienne la nuit sonne l'heure
  Les jours s'en vont je demeure

L'amour s'en va comme cette eau courante
  L'amour s'en va
 Comme la vie est lente
Et comme l'Espérance est violente

  Vienne la nuit sonne l'heure
  Les jours s'en vont je demeure

Le Pont Mirabeau

Under the pont Mirabeau flows the Seine
     Our loves flow too
  Must it recall them so
Joy came to us always after pain

     May night come and the hours ring
     The days go by and I remain

Facing each other hand in hand
     Thus we will stand
  While under our arms' bridge
Our longing looks pass in a weary band

     May night come and the hours ring
     The days go by and I remain

Love leaves us like this flowing stream
     Love flows away
  How slow life is and mild
And of how hope can suddenly run wild

     May night come and the hours ring
     The days go by and I remain

Passent les jours et passent les semaines
Ni temps passé
Ni les amours reviennent
Sous le pont Mirabeau coule la Seine

Vienne la nuit sonne l'heure
Les jours s'en vont je demeure

May the long days and the weeks go by
      Neither the past
  Nor former loves return
Under the pont Mirabeau flows the Seine

     May night come and the hours ring
     The days go by and I remain

Translated by Roger Shattuck

ROBERT DESNOS (1900–1945)

de *J'ai tant revé de toi*

J'ai tant rêvé de toi, tant marché, parlé, couché avec ton fantôme qu'il ne me reste plus peut-être, et pourtant, qu'à être fantôme parmi les fantômes et plus ombre cent fois que l'ombre qui se promène et se promènera allégrement sur le cadran solaire de ta vie.

from **I Have Dreamed So Much of You**

I have dreamed so much of you,
Walked so often, talked so often with you,
Loved your shadow so much.
Nothing is left me of you.
Nothing is left of me but a shadow among shadows,
A being a hundred times more shadowy than a shadow,
A shadowy being who comes, and comes again, in your
     sunlit life.

Translated by Kenneth Rexroth

Acknowledgments

New Directions would like to thank Mary Ann Caws, Isabella Checcaglini, Stephen Motika, Richard Sieburth, Nathaniel Weaver, and Sylvia Whitman.

Sources

Guillaume Apollinaire, "The Gypsy," "Le Pont Mirabeau," and "Wedding" from *The Selected Writings of Guillaume Apollinaire*, trans. Roger Shattuck (1971). Copyright © 1971 by Librairie Gallimard. Translation copyright © 1971 by Roger Shattuck.

Charles Baudelaire, "The Dancing Serpent," "Jewels," and "You, whom I worship as night's firmament" from *The Flowers of Evil*, ed. Marthiel and Jackson Matthews (1955, 1963, 1989). "The Dancing Serpent" translation copyright © 1989 by Barbara Gibbs. "Jewels" translation copyright © 1989 by David Paul. "You, whom I worship as night's firmament" published in *The Hudson Review*; translation copyright © 1952 by Graham Reynolds.

André Breton, "Violet Eyes" trans. Wayne Andrews, from *New Directions in Prose and Poetry 1940*. Translation copyright © 1940 by New Directions.

Claude Cahun, "Self-Love" from *Ecrits*, ed. Francois Leperlier. Copyright © 2002 by Jean-Michel Place. Translation copyright © 2016 by Mary Ann Caws.

René Char, "The Lover" and "To ***" from *Selected Poems of René Char*, ed. Mary Ann Caws and Tina Jolas. Copyright © 1988 by Éditions Gallimard. "The Lover" translation copyright © 1992 by Frederick Seidel. "To***" translation copyright © 1992 by Mark Hutchinson.